SCHOLASTIC

Math Word Problems Made Easy

Grade 3

by Bob Krech

NEW YORK • TORONTO • LONDON • AUCKLAND • SYDNEY
MEXICO CITY • NEW DELHI • HONG KONG • BUENOS AIRES

Teaching *Resources*

Dedication

To all the super elementary principals, assistant principals, and supervisors in the West Windsor-Plainsboro Schools.
Thanks for your support!

Acknowledgements

Many thanks to Jeff Grabell for his creative problem contributions

Cover design by Maria Lilja
Interior design by Holly Grundon
Interior illustrations by Mike Moran

ISBN 0-439-52971-9
Copyright © 2005 by Bob Krech
All rights reserved.
Printed in the U.S.A.

5 6 7 8 9 10   40   12 11 10 09 08 07

CONTENTS

INTRODUCTION

Problem solving is the first of the process standards listed in the *Principles and Standards for School Mathematics* (NCTM, 2000). Being selected as number one is not surprising in view of this accompanying statement from the National Council of Teachers of Mathematics (NCTM): "*Problem solving should be the central focus of all mathematics instruction and an integral part of all mathematical activity.*" In other words, in mathematics, problem solving is what it's all about.

When learning to read, we learn to recognize the letters of the alphabet, we practice letter–sound relationships, and we learn punctuation; it's all about eventually being able to read text. A similar situation exists in math. We learn how to recognize and write numerals, decipher symbols, determine numerical order, and work with operations like addition and subtraction. But it's all about what we can do with these skills—applying what we know to solve problems in daily life!

Math Word Problems Made Easy: Grade 3 is designed to help you help your students learn more about and increase their problem-solving abilities, and thus their personal math power. This book is divided into three main sections to help you:

The Fantastic Five-Step Process

The first section describes a simple five-step problem-solving process and introductory lesson you can share with your students. This process can be used with every math word problem they might encounter. This is a valuable concept to introduce at the beginning of the year and practice with students so that they will have an approach they can rely on as they encounter various types of problems.

The Super Seven Strategies

In this section, we look at the various types of problems students might encounter and the super seven strategies for approaching them. We discuss each strategy and then provide five sample problems suitable for solving with that strategy. This gives students an opportunity to practice the strategy in a context of math content appropriate to their grade level. You may want to introduce a new strategy every week or so. This way, by the end of the second month of school, students are familiar with all of the basic strategies and have had practice with them.

The Happy Hundred Word Problems

The third section is a collection of 100 math word problems focused on math concepts specific to third grade. The problems are written so students will find them fun and interesting (and maybe a little silly). No doubt about it, funny problems focus students' attention. It is much more fun and motivating for students to read about Pierre the Talking Circus Dog as he shops for a hairbrush than it is to consider when the legendary two trains will pass each other.

The problems are arranged by mathematical standard; there are sections of problems for Number and Operations, Measurement, Data Analysis and Probability, and Geometry. The individual problems are printed two to a page with a line dividing them, leaving plenty of work space for students to show their thinking. These problems can be used to introduce a concept, practice application of it, or as an end point to check for understanding.

Learning a consistent problem-solving process approach, becoming familiar with and practicing effective problem-solving strategies, and applying these ideas in word-problem contexts help students become more effective problem solvers and mathematicians. And with *Math Word Problems Made Easy: Grade 3*, they can have fun while doing it!

The Fantastic Five-Step Process

What do you do when you first encounter a math word problem? This is what we need to help students deal with. We need to help them develop a process that they can use effectively to solve any type of math word problem.

Word problems often intimidate students because there may be a lot of information; the important facts are embedded in text; and, unlike a regular equation, it is not always clear exactly what you are supposed to do. No matter what type of problem students encounter, these five steps will help them through it. Learning and using the five steps will help students *organize* their interpretation and thinking about the problem. This is the key to good problem solving—organizing for action.

The best way to help students understand the process is to demonstrate using it as you work through a problem on the board or overhead. Make a copy of the graphic organizer on page 7. You can blow this up into a poster or provide each student with his or her own copy to refer back to as you bring students through this introductory lesson.

The Fantastic Five-Step Process

What are the FACTS?

What is the QUESTION?

What can we ELIMINATE?

Choose a STRATEGY and SOLVE

Does the answer MAKE SENSE?

The Fantastic Five-Step Process

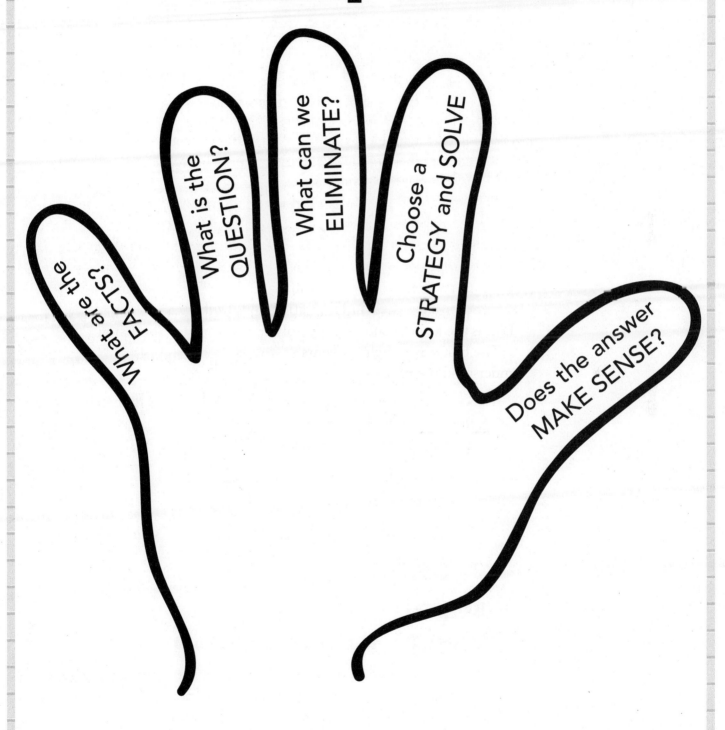

- What are the FACTS?
- What is the QUESTION?
- What can we ELIMINATE?
- Choose a STRATEGY and SOLVE
- Does the answer MAKE SENSE?

Step 1:
What Do We Know?

Begin by writing this problem on the board or overhead.

> Jock had 72 lima bean–flavored gumdrops in his
> candy jar. His brother Jack had 89. His sister,
> Jinx, had 98. Jinx said Jack had more than
> Jock. Is she right? If so, how many more?

Read the problem carefully. What are the facts? Have students volunteer these orally. Write them on the board.

> Jock had 72 gumdrops.
> Jack had 89 gumdrops.
> Jinx had 98 gumdrops.

Encourage students to write down the facts. This will help them focus on what is important while looking for ways to put it in a more accessible form. Can we arrange the facts in a way that will help us understand the problem situation? For instance, maybe it would be good to draw what we know, or put it in a list, or make a table. Sometimes it's helpful to arrange numbers from lower to higher or higher to lower, especially if we are asked to compare. Are we being asked to compare? Yes!

> Jinx – 98
> Jack – 89
> Jock – 72

Step 2:
What Do We Want to Know?

What is the question in the problem? What are we trying to find out? It is a good idea to have students state the question and also determine how the answer will be labeled. For example, if the answer is 72, then it's 72 what? 72 cats? 72 coins?

We want to know two things:
1. Was Jinx right when she said Jack had more gumdrops than Jock?
2. How many more gumdrops does Jack have than Jock?

Step 3:

What Can We Eliminate?

Once we know what we are trying to find out, we can decide what is unimportant. We may need all the information, but often there is extra information that can be put aside to help focus on the facts.

We can eliminate the fact that Jinx had 98 gumdrops. It's not needed to answer the question. We're left with

Jack – 89
Jock – 72

By comparing the numbers, we can answer the first part of the question now. Jinx was right. Jack has more.

Step 4:

Choose a Strategy or Action and Solve

Is there an action in the story (for example, is something being "taken away" or is something being "shared") that will help us decide on an operation or a way to solve the problem?

Since we have to compare something we have to find the **difference**. Usually the best way is to subtract or add up. This is the action we need to do.

$$\begin{array}{r} 89 \\ -72 \\ \hline 17 \end{array}$$

So Jack had 17 more gumdrops than Jock.

Step 5:
Does Our Answer Make Sense?

Reread the problem. Look at the answer. Is it reasonable? Is it a sensible answer given what we know?

It makes sense for several reasons. For one, 17 is a lower number than the higher number we started with. If it was higher, that would be a problem because the difference between two whole positive numbers cannot be higher than the highest number. Also, if we estimate by rounding, we see that Jack has about 90 gumdrops and Jock has about 70. The difference between 90 and 70 is 20, and 17 is pretty close to that.

Try a number of different word problems using this "talk through" format with students. You can use sample problems from throughout the book. You might invite students to try the problem themselves first and then debrief step-by-step together, sharing solutions along with you to see if all steps were considered and solutions are, in fact, correct. Practicing the process in this way helps make it part of a student's way of thinking mathematically.

The Super Seven Strategies

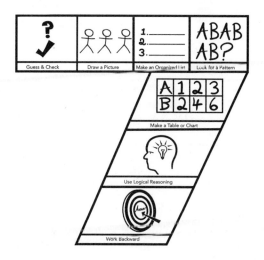

While we should encourage the use of the Five-Step Process to approach any problem, Step 4 (Choose a Strategy or Action and Solve) includes a wide range of choices. Some common strategies that are helpful to teach and practice are listed on the next few pages with sample problems. Students should have experience with all of the strategies. The more practice they have, the easier it will be for them to choose a strategy that fits the problem and helps deliver an answer.

Tip

As students learn about and practice using these strategies to solve problems, ask them to create their own problems. You can list the math concepts you want in the problems (such as addition or money) and even the strategy that must be used to solve it. Students use these parameters to create their own problems, which they can share and try out with one another. As students begin to play with these elements, their knowledge of how problems work grows, as does their confidence when encountering new problems.

Guess & Check

GUESS & CHECK

"**G**uess and Check" means if you're not sure what to do, begin with a reasonable guess to get you started. Look for key words and phrases, like "all together" or "more than," that may help move you in the right direction in choosing an operation. Students should be urged to look at the numbers in the problem and try to apply their estimation skills. This is the key to making a "reasonable" guess. Even just this first step is worth practicing. Then when a first attempted answer is arrived at, consider whether the answer is reasonable, too high, or too low. This is the "Check" part of Guess and Check.

After considering the answer, decide if you need to revise and how. Would a higher answer make sense? A lower answer? A good way to share this strategy with your class is to try one of the following problems on the board and think aloud with them through the steps. Talk out loud as you decide on your first attempt. Explain why you chose that number or numbers. Then talk to them about how you are examining the number to determine if it is reasonable. Talk about how you are adjusting your initial attempt and why.

Answers

1. 5 Mouse Morsels, 10 Tuna Surprise, and 20 Bit o' Bird

2. 5 grasshoppers and 5 starfish OR 11 starfish

3. 12 liters and 6 liters

4. 12 and 14

5. Cassie is 60 millimeters long and Claudette is 40 millimeters long

SAMPLE PROBLEMS

1. Connie the Cat was checking her pantry to see if she had enough food for the week. She found that she had 35 cans of cat food. There were twice as many cans of Tuna Surprise as there were Mouse Morsels, and twice as many cans of Bit o' Bird as there were Tuna Surprise. How many cans of Mouse Morsels, Tuna Surprise, and Bit o' Bird did Connie have?

2. Space explorer Brip just completed a mission to planet Peculiar, home to giant 6-legged grasshoppers and miniature 5-legged starfish. If Brip saw 55 legs, how many grasshoppers and starfish did he see on his mission?

3. Percy, the practical joker, has two bottles of sneeze tonic. One has 6 liters more than the other, and the two bottles have a total of 18 liters. How much sneeze tonic does each bottle contain?

4. Estelle's favorite team in the National Jacks League is the Bakersfield Buzzards. Her two favorite players are "Crusher" Curtis Craig and "Dominator" Denise Douglas. Estelle can't remember their uniform numbers but she does know that they add up to 26 and that you say one number after the other when counting by 2s. What are the two uniform numbers?

5. Cassie Cockroach and her sister Claudette together measure 100 millimeters. Cassie is 20 millimeters longer than Claudette. How long are the cockroaches?

STRATEGY 2:
Draw a Picture

DRAW A PICTURE

Drawing a picture can help answer the question in the first step of the problem-solving process: "What do we know?" Sometimes words do not easily convey the facts. Sometimes they can even confuse. By having students draw what they know, the problem can become clearer, and students can arrange and manipulate the facts more easily and discover relationships more quickly.

When students use drawings or diagrams to help solve problems, remind them that they are not creating artwork. Unnecessary details or coloring should be left out. This is also a good occasion to introduce the idea of using simple symbols to represent elements of a word problem, such as a triangle for trees or a simple stick figure for people.

Answers

1. 63 kilometers
2. 25 starships
3. 15 thornbushes
4. 2 dozen eggs
5. 28 giant cheeseburgers

SAMPLE PROBLEMS

1. Cowboy Cleon is lost in the desert. He started out yesterday riding from Saddlesore to Sidekick, a distance of 100 kilometers. 15 kilometers back, he passed a sign facing the other way that read "22 kilometers to Saddlesore." How far is he from Sidekick?

2. The starship *Knucklehead* successfully docked in the center bay of the space station *Whamo*. If there are 12 starships docked to the left of the *Knucklehead*, how many starships are visiting the space station?

3. Unfriendly Ursula is planting a circular garden designed to keep the neighbors away. She planted 5 skunk cabbages and wants to plant 3 thornbushes between each cabbage. How many thornbushes does she need?

4. Cornelius is having 7 guests over for dinner. He plans to serve his world-famous iguana egg omelet. If each person (including Cornelius) will be served an omelet using 3 eggs, how many dozen eggs does Cornelius need to buy?

5. The people of the planet Cholesterol want to build a monument in honor of Earth's greatest contribution to intergalactic civilization, the cheeseburger. They plan to put one giant cheeseburger on the highest level, 2 on the next level, 3 on the next, and so on. In all, there will be 7 levels. How many giant cheeseburgers will the monument need?

Make an Organized List

1. _____
2. _____
3. _____
_____

MAKE AN ORGANIZED LIST

"**M**ake an Organized List" is a strategy that helps us identify and organize what we know. In problems where, for example, combinations must be determined, listing all possible combinations is essential. Compiling a list can help students see if they have considered all possibilities. Lists, as well as drawings, can also help reveal patterns that may exist.

As an introduction to this strategy it may be helpful for students to use or make manipulatives as they create their lists of data. For example, if you ask students to find all the possible combinations of shorts and T-shirts when you have a red T-shirt, a green T-shirt, a white pair of shorts, and a pink pair of shorts, you might have them use colored cubes to represent the clothes, or color and cut out some simple drawings of the clothes. Students can then list each combination of manipulatives.

Answers

1. 12 costumes

2. Four combinations (3 3-liter bottles and 1 1-liter bottle OR 2 3-liter and 4 1-liter bottles OR 1 3-liter and 7 1-liter bottles OR 10 1-liter bottles)

3. 20 washcloths

4. Six ways (1 toffee, 1 bar, and 4 drops OR 1 toffee and 9 drops OR 3 bars and 4 drops OR 2 bars and 9 drops OR 1 bar and 14 drops OR 19 drops)

5. 6 games

SAMPLE PROBLEMS

1. Clifford the Clown is selecting his costume for a highly paid job to entertain at 4-year-old Regina's birthday party. He has 4 wigs to choose from (rainbow, hot pink, teal, and bald) and 3 different noses (red and fat, green and pointy, and yellow and runny). How many different costumes can he make if each costume is made up of one wig and one nose?

2. Renata Wren is quite a snob, so only the finest imported sparkling water is good enough to fill her birdbath. Her birdbath holds 10 liters of water. The water is sold in 3-liter and 1-liter bottles. How many combinations of 3- and 1-liter bottles can she buy to fill her birdbath? (While fussy, Renata isn't wasteful. She uses all the water in the bottles for her bird bath.)

3. The 5 dwarves (cousins to those other dwarves) have decided to form a washcloth exchange club. Crabby, Itchy, Lazy, Cozy, and Heavy have agreed that they will each give a colorful and functional washcloth to the other 4 members of the club. How many washcloths will be exchanged at the first meeting?

4. Little Lenny Looper has 19 cents burning a hole in his pocket. He has decided to spend it all on candy. He can buy asparagus toffee for 10 cents, sea-urchin bars for 5 cents, and lime slime drops for a penny. How many different ways can Lenny spend his money?

5. The Extreme Tag League (XTL) will begin playing next year with teams in 4 cities: Baltimore Bats, Los Angeles Lizards, Philadelphia Flies, and Seattle Snails. If each team plays the others once, how many games will be played in the first season?

STRATEGY 4:
Look for a Pattern

ABAB
AB?
_____

LOOK FOR A PATTERN

Using lists and drawing pictures help reveal patterns that may exist within the information a problem supplies. The guiding question for discovering patterns is, "What relationships do you see between the numbers in the problem?" How far apart are they from each other? Do they increase or decrease by certain amounts in certain ways? Asking these questions will often lead to a good solution.

In a problem where we are told that Surelook lived at 222 Beaker Street and that his next-door neighbor on his left lived at 220, we could use a pattern to tell what the address of the person living on his right, two doors down would be (226). Number lines, hundred charts, and calculators can be useful tools in helping students recognize a pattern that may exist in a problem.

Answers

1. 4 rounds
2. 8 pictures
3. 11 (plus 1, plus 2, plus 3, etc.)
4. 5 (it's a pentagon)
5. 32 kilograms

SAMPLE PROBLEMS

1. Sophie Squirrel is organizing a nut-eating tournament. 16 squirrels are scheduled to compete. The winner of each match goes on to the next round and the loser goes home. How many rounds will it take to finish the tournament?

2. Cyrus is publishing a new book, *My Favorite Fungi*. To keep expenses down, the publisher will be printing full-color pictures only on every fifth page (starting with page 5.) If the book is 44 pages long, how many pictures will the book have?

3. At the urging of her friends, Millicent started selling her famous sardine pies to the public. On Monday she sold one pie; on Tuesday she sold 2 pies; on Wednesday she sold 4; and on Thursday she sold 7. If the pattern continues, how many pies will she sell on Friday?

4. Fashionable Fiona bought a necklace from one of the finest designers in town. Hanging from the necklace are jewels shaped like triangles, squares, and pentagons. The jewels follow a pattern: triangle, square, pentagon. How many sides will the 30th jewel have?

5. Apprentice Wizard Wally accidentally cast a spell on his pet rat Ricky. On Monday, before the spell was cast, Ricky weighed one kilogram (he was a fat rat). On Tuesday, Ricky weighed 2 kilograms. On Wednesday, he weighed 4 kilograms, and he blew up to 8 kilograms on Thursday. How much did Ricky weigh on Saturday?

Make a Table or Chart

Here's another strategy that helps organize information and thus better answer the first question in the problem-solving process: "What do we know?" Tables or charts are a way to organize two groups of data to better see what the relationship between the two groups might be. It helps make patterns and functions that create patterns more apparent.

For example, if we know that one can of beans costs 5¢, 2 cans are 10¢, and 3 cans are 15¢, by creating a table with this information, students will be able to figure out how much 8 cans of beans would cost (40¢). The table organizes the quantity and the cost so it's easier to see the relationship. As students use tables and charts, caution them as to how far to extend the data. In the case of the problem above, all we need to know is how much 8 cans cost. It wouldn't make sense to extend the table to 10 cans because that would be adding extra work and more information than we need.

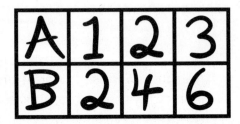

MAKE A TABLE OR CHART

Answers

1. 25 meters

2. 5 ways (4 packages of 5 servings and 3 boxes of single servings OR 3 packages of 5s and 8 boxes of singles OR 2 packages of 5s and 13 boxes of singles OR 1 package of 5s and 18 boxes of singles OR 23 boxes of singles)

3. 5 packages

4. 10:15 P.M.

5. 16 pieces of lint

SAMPLE PROBLEMS

1. Science enthusiast Lulu has decided to perform an important experiment. She dropped her father's expensive new watch from the roof of her building, which is 400 meters tall. After the watch hit the pavement the first time, it bounced up 200 meters. After the second bounce, it rose 100 meters. If the pattern continues, how high will the watch rise in the fourth bounce?

2. Clarence, the canine chef, has perfected a new specialty for his furry friends, dog-food ravioli. The raviolis can be bought in boxes with a single serving or in packages with 5 servings. If you wanted to buy 23 servings, how many ways could you do it?

3. Broccoli cookies are sold six per package:

Number of Packages	1	2	3	4	5
Number of Cookies	6	12	18		

How many packages must be purchased to have 30 cookies?

4. The Flipping Lids, this year's hottest band, will be playing at Chunky Chester's all weekend. On Saturday night, they will play 3 shows. Each show lasts for 45 minutes and will be followed by a 30-minute break. If the Lids start flipping at 7:00 P.M., when will they finish?

5. Morton has a fine collection of 12 rare bagpipes but has grown bored with his hobby. After searching for a new interest, he decided to start collecting lint. Tillie, who has a large lint collection, has agreed to trade with him. She will give 4 choice pieces of lint for every 3 bagpipes. If Morton trades all his bagpipes, how many pieces of lint will he receive?

STRATEGY 6:
Use Logical Reasoning

USE LOGICAL REASONING

Logical reasoning is an approach that organizes and analyzes information so that it ultimately leads to a conclusion. Ideas that help students think logically include using lists, pictures, tables, charts, and looking for patterns. A logic matrix and Venn diagram are also helpful tools in organizing information in a logical way and seeing possibilities.

A logic matrix can help us organize facts and use the process of elimination to arrive at an answer. For example, "Jim lives in a blue house and drinks milk. Bert does not live in a green house. The person in the white house drinks juice. Joan drinks water. Where does Bert live?"

Person	House	Drink
Bert		Juice
Joan	Green	Water
Jim	Blue	Milk

Venn diagrams are also very useful for organizing information and supporting logical reasoning. For example, "The Eatalotsky family hosted Thanksgiving. There was a choice of main courses: turkey, ham, or both. Seven of the family members had turkey. Seven had ham. Since there are ten Eatalotskys, how many had both ham and turkey?" The Venn diagram helps provide an answer.

Dinner

Ham   Turkey

Answers

1. Jane
2. Julius was shrunk to the size of a hamster, Virgil was turned into pudding, Romulus glowed in the dark, and Cicero developed an intense appetite for guacamole.
3. 2 customers
4. a triangle
5. 55 grubs

SAMPLE PROBLEMS

1. Wayne, Lane, Jane, and Horatio all ran for the office of Supreme Commander of the Duck, Duck, Goose Club. Horatio had more votes than Wayne but fewer than Jane. Wayne received more votes than Lane. Who was elected Supreme Commander?

2. Aspiring witch Wynona cast 4 different spells on 4 classmates but can't remember which spell was cast on whom. Romulus was not turned into pudding. Julius was shrunk to the size of a hamster. Virgil neither glowed in the dark nor developed an intense appetite for guacamole. Cicero did not glow in the dark. Which spell was cast on whom?

3. It was the first day of business for Edwina's new cottage-cheese-and-toppings stand, and she decided to give away free samples. 15 new customers were given a free bowl of cottage cheese with a choice of 2 toppings. If she served 9 bowls with licorice topping and 8 with horseradish, how many customers picked both licorice and horseradish?

4. Ida, Ada, and Edie have built habitats for their pet anteaters. Ida's habitat has 2 more sides than Ada's and 3 less than Edie's. If Edie's habitat has 8 sides, what shape is Ada's?

5. Leticia is the proud owner of the Circle Q Grub Ranch. The number of grubs on the ranch is an odd number that is more than 50 and less than 100. You say the number when you count by 5s. The sum of the digits in the tens and ones places equals 10. How many grubs does Leticia have on her ranch?

Work Backward

WORK BACKWARD

Working backward is a good strategy to employ when we know how a problem ends up, but we don't know how it started. For example, if I went to the store and bought a hammer for $2.50 and the clerk gave me $2.50 change, how much money did I give the clerk to begin with? It is still a matter of applying the Five-Step Process and organizing information first, but the trick here is to know where to begin and to think about using inverse operations.

These types of problems are a great opportunity to help students see the usefulness of using letters or symbols to represent unknown quantities. For example, with the hammer problem we could think:

> I gave the clerk x. And since I got back $2.50 and the hammer costs $2.50, then $2.50 + $2.50 = x.
>
> x = $5.00

Answers

1. 400 copies
2. 8 meters each
3. 12 kilograms of anchovies
4. 45 minutes
5. 5 slugs

SAMPLE PROBLEMS

1. Leonard's music store has been selling record numbers of the new hit CD *Wood, You Eat It!* by The Termites. On Thursday, the first shipment of CDs arrived. On Friday, Leonard sold 90 copies. On Saturday, he sold 130. On Sunday, he sold 60 copies and had 120 left at the end of the day. How many copies arrived on Thursday?

2. Sherwood needs to build a rectangular pen to hold his pet worm Wesley. If the area of the pen measures 72 square meters and two sides measure 9 meters each, how long are each of the other two sides?

3. Clyde's recipe for pound-cake topping calls for one kilogram of fudge and 2 kilograms of anchovies. Clyde has a big order and has to make 18 kilograms of topping. How many kilograms of anchovies does he need?

4. Daphne and Desiree played together for 3 hours. They played Catch the Armadillo for an hour and 15 minutes, juggled pineapples for an hour, and wrestled pigs for the rest of the time. How much time did they spend wrestling pigs?

5. Jacobina predicts that she will find 50 slugs in a bag containing 100 worms, beetles, and slugs. She based her prediction on her experience with a bag of 10 critters that had the same ratio of worms, beetles, and slugs. How many slugs did Jacobina find in the smaller bag?

The Happy Hundred Word Problems

100

The "Happy Hundred Word Problems" are organized by the NCTM content standards. Within each standard section, problems are further organized and labeled by the major math concepts typically found in third-grade math curriculums. For example, Number and Operations is a large standard that includes concepts like place value, money, addition, and subtraction. There are specific word problems here for each of these concepts. The concept focus is marked in the upper left-hand corner of each problem. The answers are provided in the answer key on pp. 77–79.

As you introduce a problem, remind students to use the Five-Step Process. Keep the graphic organizer prominently displayed on a poster or chart, or give students a copy of their own to refer to. On each page you will find two problems with space for students to show their thinking. Encourage students to write down their solution process including any words, numbers, pictures, diagrams, or tables they use. This helps students with their thinking and understanding of the problem, while giving you more assessment information.

When assessing students' work on word problems, two major aspects need consideration: process and product. Observe students as they work on or discuss problems. Focus on what they say, and whether they use manipulatives, pictures, computation on scrap paper, or other strategies. When looking at their written products consider what skills they are exhibiting as well as what errors or misunderstandings they may be showing. This is why it is essential that students "show their thinking" as they solve a problem and explain their rationale.

Finally, have fun! These problems are designed to appeal to kids' sense of humor. Enjoy the situations and the process. Using what they know to solve word problems gives students a sense of mastery, accomplishment, meaning, and math power!

NUMBER AND OPERATIONS
PLACE VALUE, MONEY, AND TIME

1 Place Value Through Hundreds

There are strange insects on Planet Zoog. Strange, but fast! The Pizbot can fly between 100 and 200 miles per hour. The Waztail flies from 150 to 250 miles per hour. The Gerzix flies between 150 and 195 miles per hour. One of these insects recently flew 410 miles in 2 hours. Which one was it?

2 Place Value Through Thousands

Barney is a good salesman. He sold thousands of chocolate-covered mosscakes on his last sales trip. He sold 4,503 cases in Peoria, 5,304 cases in Abilene, 4,353 in Wilmington, and 5,043 in Little Rock. Anytime he sells more than 4,500 cases in a city he gets a bonus of $1,000. How much bonus money did he earn on this trip?

Comparing and Ordering Numbers

It was a close finish in the Annual Toaster Throwing Championship. Lisa Musclesworth heaved the toaster 1,414 inches. Pat Pernicious threw 70 inches farther than Lisa. Belinda Bigenough's best throw was 1,408 inches. Who's the winner?

Rounding Numbers to Tens

Dragstrip Eddie is driving through Transylvania. It's late and all the gas stations are closed. He sees on a mileage marker that he is 106 miles from Batston, 165 miles from Wolfbane Borough, and 176 miles from Dracaville. He's got enough gas in his tank to go another 150 miles. Where do you think he should head for tonight?

Rounding Numbers to Hundreds

Dr. Wacky is using his time-travel machine again. He wants to visit the inventor of the two-man kazoo. The two-man kazoo was invented in 1902. The time-travel machine is not exact, but he wants to get as close as possible. Should he set his approximator dial to the year 1906, 1916, 1950, or 1899?

Place Value Through Hundred Thousands

Little Goldy is going to get $500,000 for his birthday from Uncle Big Bucks. He's saved $60,000 already from his very successful lemonade stand. Since he is turning 12, his parents have also decided to give him a $100 bill for every year of his life. How much money will he have?

7 Comparing and Ordering Greater Numbers

Mack, Mick, Mika, and Moki are pinball wizards and avid bike riders. Their pinball tournament scores were awesome. Mack has a red bike. The player with the blue bike scored 417,363. Mick scored 407,363 and has a purple bike. A player with a bike that is neither blue nor green scored 500,001. Moki scored 407,363 and has a green bike. Mack claimed he was the winner. Was he right?

8 Rounding Greater Numbers

Talk about big collections! Yigzat from Planet Flop collects dust specks. She has 347,999 specks. Her brother, Bassinet, asked her about how many dust specks she has. What would be her best answer to the nearest hundred thousand?

Math Word Problems Made Easy: Grade 3 · Scholastic Teaching Resources

Compare Money Amounts

Chuck delivers *The Daily Blab* in his neighborhood. It is collection day on Chuck's paper route. He went to three houses. He got a $5 bill, a $1 bill, and a penny from Mr. Yawn. He got two $1 bills and 4 quarters from Mrs. Yap. He got two $5 bills and a half-dollar from Ms. Yelp. Who paid Chuck the most money? How much?

Time

The Blah Network is showing some great new television shows. Penrod's new favorite is *Wallpaper Weekly*. It starts at 9:15 A.M. The show itself lasts 75 minutes, but there are two 2-minute commercials and four 30-second commercials in there also. What time is it over?

Time

The Whiz is a fabulously fast superhero. But if he's going to save Lois Loon from evil Dr. Napkin he will have to get to Dr. Napkin's hideout by midnight. It is 9:05 P.M. now. He has to pick up his laundry from his mother's first, but that will take only half an hour. How long does The Whiz have to get to the hideout from his mother's house?

Estimating Sums

Edgar was planning a trip to Couscous City. If the trip was more than 100 miles he figured he would take the train. Anything less, he decided he would use his pogo stick. He looked at a map and saw that it was about 32 miles to Riceville. From Riceville to Couscous City was another 57 miles. Estimate the mileage. Should Edgar take the train or the pogo stick?

Math Word Problems Made Easy: Grade 3   Scholastic Teaching Resources

13   Adding Two-Digit Numbers

Chef Crayzee was making his infamous pie à la bug. His special recipe called for 41 black ants, 52 beetles, 29 mealworms, 27 red ants, and 16 flies to make one batch. How many ants does he need to make two batches?

14   Adding Two-Digit Numbers

Wally and Wilhemina, the Wolverine Twins, got a total of 80 presents at their birthday party. Wally got 2 more presents than Wilhemina. How many presents did Wilhemina get?

15 Adding Two-Digit Numbers With Regrouping

There are 55 peanuts in each Nutto Bar. There are 31 peanuts in each Diet Nutto Bar. There are 17 peanuts in each Junior Nutto Bar. There are 14 peanuts in a Mini-Junior Nutto Bar. If you ate 72 peanuts, which two candy bars did you eat?

16 Adding Three-Digit Numbers

Uncle Chapeau arrived at a birthday party wearing 479 hats. He tried to get through the front door but couldn't, so he removed 128 hats. He tried again, but still couldn't make it through. He took off another 237 hats and just squeezed through. How many hats did he take off?

17 · Adding Four-Digit Numbers

Diver Dana is going down into the dangerous depths of the Doughnutian Sea. She dove down 1,735 feet. She rested there and photographed a school of rare Elmo fish. She then continued another 8,134 feet till she reached the bottom. How deep is the bottom?

18 · Adding Three Addends

Zip, Zap, and Zoop have entered themselves as a team in the third annual Cotton Ball Olympics. In order for a team to get to the final round, they must have a team total of 1,000 points. Zip scored 94 points. Zap scored 62 points. Zoop scored 845 points. They had one point deducted from their total for poor sportsmanship when Zip bit the referee. Did they make it to the finals?

19 Extending Addition: Money

Magpie is selling homemade cucumber juice. He charges $5 for a gallon or 50¢ for a cup. He made $15 on Monday and sold 4 gallons on Tuesday. How much money did he make in all?

20 Extending Addition: Money

Sidney Squirrel had only 14¢ in his bank account. Fortunately, he is good at finding change. He found 4 dimes, 2 quarters, 5 nickels, 4 acorns, 2 pennies, and a shoelace. He deposited it all into his account. How much money does he have in the bank now?

21   Extending Addition: Money

Minky told George, "I have 68 cents in my pocket. I have a quarter, 4 nickels, 3 pennies, and 2 other coins. If you can guess what the other two coins are, I'll give you half the money."

   George said, "You have a nickel and a dime." Should George get half the money?

22   Using Dollars and Cents

Penrod was counting his coin collection. He had a stack of 18 shiny new quarters. Mr. Slick happened by and said, "Tell you what, my boy. You give me those quarters and I'll give you a brand-new $5 bill." Should Penrod do it?

23   Adding Larger Money Amounts

Rapunzel is very excited about toeball season starting. She rushed out to buy her new equipment. She bought a new pair of regulation toeball socks for $3.99, two toeguards for 59¢ each, and a practice ball for $9.09. How much did she spend all together?

24   Making Change

The menu at Chez Dawg is pretty irresistible. Pettina Poodle orders a platter of bones for $2.53, a side order of kibble for $1.25, and a large bowl of water for $0.75. She gives the clerk a $5 bill. How much change should she get?

25   Subtraction

Jim is a dedicated Beaver Scout. He is on his way to summer camp. He has 4 merit badges from last year and he earned 5 merit badges this year. In order to attain the rank of Eager Beaver he must have 17 merit badges by the end of camp. He usually earns 2 badges a week. Camp lasts 4 weeks. Can he become an Eager Beaver this summer? Why or why not?

26   Subtraction

Cremora Crackup is giving away her collection of 58 rare and exotic paper clips. She has given 15 to her niece, Nestley, and 15 to her nephew, Nastley. If she does the same for her cousin, Cookie, how many paper clips will Cremora have left?

27

Estimating Differences Using Rounding

Cosmo had 722 marbles ready for the big marble show. He had a hole in his pocket and lost 302 of them. He needs 400 to enter the show. Does he still have enough to enter?

28

Subtracting With Regrouping

The Martian exploratory force had 65 crew members. On the way to Earth they took a rest stop on the moon. 17 Martians stayed too long in the restroom and missed the rocket to Earth. How many Martians are on the rocket?

29 — Subtracting Three-Digit Numbers

Gina and Joanie are having a braid-growing contest. Gina's braid is 195 inches. It took her 232 days to grow it. Joanie's braid is 81 inches. It took her 228 days to grow it. How much longer is Gina's braid than Joanie's?

30 — Subtracting With Two Regroupings

The Super Colossal Double Dynamite pack of bubble gum has 444 pieces. Erwin said he could chew every piece of it in less than a week. So far he has chewed 159 pieces in three days. How many more pieces does he have to chew to finish the pack?

31 **Subtracting Across Zero**

Louie, Dewey, and Gooey went to the store to buy snacks. Their mother gave each of them a $5 bill. Louie spent $1.77. Dewey spent $2.35. Gooey spent $2.17. Who got $2.83 in change?

32 **Subtracting Four-Digit Numbers**

The folks on Planet Splinx live a l-o-o-o-n-n-g time. The oldest man there is Kanu Seemee. He's 4,537 years old. His brother Ukan is only 2,913 years old. How much older is Kanu than Ukan?

33 Subtracting Money

Irresponsible Ira rented a pickle-making machine. It costs $1.50 a day to rent. Ira paid $4.50 for three days rental and a $10.00 deposit to make sure he returned the machine. For every day the machine is late being returned, $1.75 is subtracted from the deposit. Ira returned the machine after having it for 6 days. How much of his deposit did he get back?

34 Multiplication

Super Sticky Sour Spots come in strips of 5. Sally buys 4 strips. She wants to give one Sour Spot to each of her 19 hermit crabs. Will she have enough?

35 Multiplication

The Yinx is an unusual bird. It flies 7 miles a day, but it flies only on days that begin with the letter "T" or "S." How far does the Yinx fly in 3 weeks?

36 Multiplication

Nixie opened her lemonade stand on Monday. She sold 4 cups of lemonade that day. On Tuesday she sold 6 cups and on Wednesday she sold 8 cups. If this pattern continues, how many cups of lemonade do you think she will sell on Saturday?

37 **Multiplication With Zero**

If you play Uncle Oscar's Lucky Dart Game you can win big! If you hit the nose on the Uncle Oscar target you get 10 points. If you hit an ear, you get 5 points. If you hit the hat you get 1 point. If you hit any other part you get 0 points. Mickey threw three darts. He hit the hair, the thumb, and the bow tie. How many points did he score all together?

38 **Multiplication**

Wayne eats 9 bowls of Yummie-O's a day. He does this for 4 days. Wanda eats 5 bowls of Yummie-O's a day. She does this for 8 days. Who eats the most Yummie-O's?

39   Multiplication

Doodlewazzers have 3 eyes on each of their 4 heads. Fangwanglers have 7 eyes on each of their 2 heads. How many eyes do 3 Doodlewazzers and 3 Fangwanglers have all together?

40   Division

Garzoovians have arrived from space! Peeking under the spaceship you can see their legs. There are 24 legs. You know Garzoovians have 3 legs each. How many Garzoovians are there?

Math Word Problems Made Easy: Grade 3   Scholastic Teaching Resources

41 Multiplication With Three Factors

You are taking care of your neighbor's pet stinkbugs, Mel and Molly. They each get 2 vitamin drops per day. How many vitamin drops will you have used after 5 days?

42 Division

Pez is a nice guy. When he got 16 chocolate-covered squid for his birthday, he was ready to share them equally with his 3 brothers. How many chocolate-covered squid should each brother get?

 **Division**

There were 18 space explorers. They were getting ready to explore 6 planets. There were 2 space explorers in each spacecraft. How many spacecraft were there?

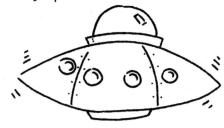

 **Division**

Renaldo made a super pepperoni-and-sour-cream sandwich for his cooking-class graduation party. It is 4 feet long. He cut it into 16 pieces. If each person gets 2 pieces, how many people can Renaldo serve?

Math Word Problems Made Easy: Grade 3 · Scholastic Teaching Resources

45 — Connecting Multiplication and Division

In order to win the Pawxatawny Peanut Brittle Championship, Darwin must have a perfect score of 25. During the competition he must make 5 batches of peanut brittle. The judges will then score each batch and total the scores. What is the maximum score possible for each batch?

46 — Dividing by 5

Little Pizbo is organizing a league for that hot new sport, Crazyball. Each Crazyball team has these positions: left flipper, right flipper, center flipper, back flipper, and forward flipper. 40 players signed up for the new Crazyball League. How many teams can Little Pizbo put together?

Dividing by 6 and 7

Rodney Rooster's Roasted Rice Balls are a big hit! Rodney got an order over the phone for 3 medium-sized gift boxes. He packed up 21 rice balls into the 3 boxes. How many rice balls were in each box?

Dividing by 8 and 9

Sidney Savant has invented a new game—Sidnarama. It has a board with 72 squares lined up in rows. Each row has 8 squares. The board has a perimeter of 34 inches. How many rows are there on the board?

49 — Multiplying by Tens/ Exploring Multiplication Patterns

At the Better Big Bug Exhibition, Rozwell said, "I've got 4 rows of bugs with 5 bugs in each row."

Insectiva said, "I've got 4 rows with 50 bugs in each row."

Arachnid said, "Not bad, but I have 4 rows with 500 bugs in each row."

How many bugs does each contestant have?

50 — Estimating Products

There are 315 members of the Merry Martian Marching Society. They are going to play in the Venusian Battle of the Bands Contest. They need to rent spacecraft to get them there. Each spacecraft is 220 feet long and holds 110 passengers. Will 2 spacecraft be enough for the band?

51 Multiplication: Partial Products

Marvin was building tricycles for his pet shrimp. He had 17 shrimp. He wanted to buy wheels. He figured he would have to multiply 17 by 3. His sister, Merva said, "An easy way to do that is just multiply 7 x 3 and get 14. Then multiply 10 x 3 and get 30. Add them together and you have 44!" Is Merva right? Why or why not?

52 Multiplying Two-Digit Numbers

Jingo needs 245 helmets for the army ants in his ant farm. The helmets are sold in packs of 5, 6, or 7 helmets. Should Jingo buy 39 five-packs, 38 six-packs, or 35 seven-packs?

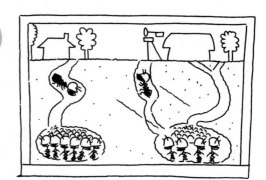

53 — Multiplying Two-Digit Numbers

A train ticket to go from East Boogaloo to West Boogaloo costs $13. Shaggy wants to buy tickets for himself, his younger twin brothers, and his cousins, the Tornado triplets. How much money will he need?

54 — Multiplying Three-Digit Numbers

Oceana rented a fishing boat. She wanted to take some of her pet water buffalo with her. Each water buffalo weighs 455 pounds. The boat can hold 2,000 pounds. Oceana weighs 55 pounds. How many of her pet water buffalo can she bring with her?

55 Multiplying Three-Digit Numbers

Gerald Giant, who happens to live at the top of a beanstalk, wears a big sneaker. It's 320 inches long. His friend, Enormous Ed, wears one that's 4 times as big. How big is Enormous Ed's sneaker?

56 Multiplying Money

The new book for kids, *100 Ways to Annoy Your Teacher*, was just released. It is quickly becoming a best-seller. One copy costs $1.97. Mendacious Moe buys 5 copies. Because his brother works in the bookstore he gets 50¢ off each copy. How much did he spend?

Division

The Dingle family rented an electric turkey for 360 minutes. All the Dingles want to play with it. Dad Dingle said, "Everybody will take turns and get an even amount of time with the turkey." There are 6 Dingles who want to play. How many minutes does each one get?

Dividing With Remainders

There were 5 players on the Ypsilanti Yardbirds no-contact yarnball team. The Yardbirds won a tournament recently and were awarded 44 yellow yo-yos. How many yo-yos should each Yardbird get? Will there be any left over?

59   Dividing With Remainders

Chef Zoidsterona was making her famous Intergalactic Muffins. She bought 25 Plutonian peaches to make half a dozen muffins. When she was done she had one peach left over. How many peaches went into each muffin?

60   Exploring Equal Parts

The cake-decorating class was going well. Icing was everyone's favorite part. Boris's cake has $\frac{1}{2}$ blue and $\frac{1}{2}$ red icing. Belinda's cake has $\frac{1}{3}$ red, $\frac{1}{3}$ green, and $\frac{1}{3}$ blue icing. Bobby's cake has $\frac{1}{4}$ red, $\frac{1}{4}$ blue, $\frac{1}{4}$ white, and $\frac{1}{4}$ green icing. Whose cake has the most green icing?

Math Word Problems Made Easy: Grade 3 · Scholastic Teaching Resources

61 — Exploring Equivalent Fractions

Kenyatta Cupcake made 5 fruitcakes, all the same size. Ziggy had $\frac{5}{10}$ of a lemon fruitcake. He wanted to trade it for an equal amount of lizard-flavored fruitcake. Mishy had $\frac{1}{2}$ of a lizard-flavored fruitcake and Moshy had $\frac{2}{3}$ of one. Who should Ziggy trade with to have a fair trade?

62 — Comparing and Ordering Fractions

Seaweed King Restaurant was giving out free sesame seaweed snack bars. Pip had $\frac{2}{8}$ of a bar. Pop had $\frac{4}{12}$ of a bar. Pap had $\frac{1}{6}$ of a bar. Pep had $\frac{1}{2}$ of a bar. Who had the smallest piece?

63   Fractions and Sets

Elvis Entropy bought a pack of Famous Amoeba collector cards. There are 12 cards in a pack. He gave 3 cards to his sister, Elvira, and 4 to his friend, Enos. What fraction of the pack is left?

64   Finding a Fraction of a Number

The olive-throwing competition began with Amanda Mananda in first place. She hit 8 out of 27 targets. Miranda Ramanda went next. 27 targets were thrown into the air. She hit $\frac{1}{3}$ of them. Should Miranda be in first place? Why or why not?

Math Word Problems Made Easy: Grade 3   Scholastic Teaching Resources

65 Mixed Numbers

No one makes toenail pie like Aunt Yuck. She slices her pies into 8 slices each. For the last Yuck family get-together she made 2 pies. There were $1\frac{5}{8}$ pies left at the end of the party. Aunt Yuck was the only one who ate any. How many slices did she eat?

66 Adding and Subtracting Fractions

Little Lenny loves drinking Jolly Juice. His mother gave him a full bottle at breakfast to last him the day. He had $\frac{1}{3}$ of the bottle at breakfast. If he drinks $\frac{1}{3}$ of the bottle at lunch, how much will he have drunk?

Adding and Subtracting Fractions

The Tennessee Termites were playing the Minnesota Mealworms in the All-Insect Bowl. Coach Thorax told Max that he would let him play $\frac{3}{4}$ of the game. So far he has played $\frac{1}{4}$. How much more of the game will Max play?

Tenths: Fractions and Decimals

The Junior Scholastic Finger Skateboard Final 500-Centimeter Sprint turned out to be very close. Jack's time was 7 seconds. Jock's time was $\frac{2}{10}$ of a second less. Jekyll's time was 6.6 seconds. Who won the race?

69 Hundredths: Fractions and Decimals

At the Annual Ant Olympics, Sydney Sixleg was favored to win the diving-into-a-thimble competition. He got three dives and his scores were 9.25, 9.05, and 9.5. His rival, Ivan Insectalovich, had scores of 9.15, 9.51, and 9.1. Who had the highest single score? What was it?

70 Adding and Subtracting Decimals

Chef Cynthia Scaldini was making her famous five-alarm hot sauce. Her recipe calls for 1.8 oz of vinegar, 0.5 oz of cayenne-pepper sauce, and 0.3 oz of horseradish. Should she put it in the 2.2-oz jar or the 2.6-oz jar?

71 Adding and Subtracting Decimals

Rodney Rodent has 25.7 pounds of the highly prized Stinkmeister cheese. He gives his cousin Ralph 13.9 pounds. He then gets hungry and eats 5.5 pounds himself. How much cheese does he have left?

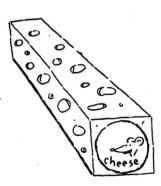

72 Decimals and Money

Penny Petlover went Christmas shopping for her pets. She spent $1.49 on a new leash for her turkey. She bought a sweater for her hermit crab that was on sale for $1.99. Finally she couldn't resist getting her salamander a paint-by-number set for $1.35. She gave the clerk a $5 bill. How much change should she get?

Math Word Problems Made Easy: Grade 3 Scholastic Teaching Resources

73 — Exploring Length

The Evansville Earthworm Extravaganza was great. The contest for longest earthworm was won by Edgar Eligible's pet earthworm, Bruno. Bruno was 3 inches less than a foot in length and 2 inches wide. How long was Bruno?

74 — Measuring to the Nearest $\frac{1}{2}$ and $\frac{1}{4}$ Inch

Detailed Dora was measuring the buttons on her coat. She wanted each button to be exactly 2 inches wide. One of the buttons she measured was $\frac{1}{2}$ inch less than that. She replaced it. How wide was the button she replaced?

Measuring to the Nearest $\frac{1}{2}$ and $\frac{1}{4}$ Inch

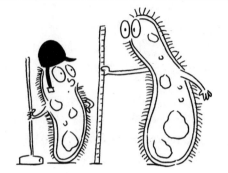

To play on the Minuscule Microbes Polo Team you must be at least $3\frac{3}{4}$ inches tall. Peanut Paramecium wants to join the team. He was measured at the tryouts and found to be $2\frac{1}{2}$ inches tall. How much taller must he be before he can play on the team?

Exploring Length in Feet and Inches

Rex is working in metal shop class. His final project is to make the world's largest letter opener. It has to be 49 inches long. His teacher said he could provide Rex with 4 pieces of metal to use. Each one is one foot in length. Will that be enough for Rex's project?

77 — Inches, Feet, and Yards

The Exotic Grass and Weed Convention was almost over. The final contest was for the longest piece of dried grass. Sylvester had one that was 39 inches long. Socrates had one that was 1 yard* long. Saliver had one that was 3 feet and 2 inches long. Who won first place? second? third?

* 1 yard = 3 feet

78 — Centimeters and Decimeters

The inhabitants of Planet Bitsy are not very tall. The Bitsy City Bacon Bits have the three tallest players in the NBA (National Bitsyball Association). Sam Squig is 11 centimeters tall. Alvin Arg is 1 decimeter* tall. Cletus Clamshaw is twice as tall as his little brother, Clankus, who is 6.5 centimeters tall. Who is the tallest player?

* 1 decimeter = 10 centimeters

79 Meters and Centimeters

"Get the one that's 1 meter* long," said Binky. He was looking through the Titanic Toothbrush catalog with his brother, Pinky.

Pinky said, "I'm thinking about getting 3 of these 35-centimeter ones and just duct-taping them together to make one big toothbrush." Which toothbrush would be bigger?

* 1 meter = 100 centimeters

80 Capacity: Customary Units

Count Drinkula must drink 3 pints* of his favorite beverage, tomato juice, before the sun rises. So far he has had 5 cups of tomato juice. The sun will rise in one hour. How much more does he need to drink?

* 1 pint = 2 cups

Math Word Problems Made Easy: Grade 3 Scholastic Teaching Resources

81   Capacity: Metric Units

The water fountain is leaking! Mr. Yak's third-grade class comes to the rescue. They find that the water is leaking at the rate of 190 milliliters* per minute. The custodian says he can stop the leak in 5 minutes. Until then the third graders must collect the water as it leaks out. Will a liter bottle be enough to collect all the leaking water?

* 1,000 milliliters = 1 liter

82   Weight: Customary Units

"I weigh more than that watermelon," said Peanut.
   "No, you don't," said Petunia. "You weigh only 64 ounces*. That watermelon weighs 6 pounds." Who is right?

* 16 ounces = 1 pound

Weight: Metric Units

Aunt Gummy's chocolate-covered bricks are not as popular as she had hoped. She has 10 bricks left over after her big closeout sale. Each brick weighs 900 grams*. The disposal company told her they would haul away any leftover bricks but would charge her $1.50 per kilogram. How much will it cost her to get rid of the leftover bricks?

* 1,000 grams = 1 kilogram

Temperature

Freaky Fred's Fantastic Fruit-Flavored Fizzie Fluid freezes at 45° Fahrenheit. It boils at 55° Fahrenheit. It is 32° Fahrenheit in Wancouver, 41° Fahrenheit in Mancouver, and 50° Fahrenheit in Stancouver. Where should Fred go to enjoy drinking his fabulous fluid?

Math Word Problems Made Easy: Grade 3 · Scholastic Teaching Resources

DATA ANALYSIS AND PROBABILITY

85 — Bar Graphs

The kids in Mr. Yazoo's third-grade class at East Doughnut Elementary were voting on a new school song. This graph shows the results of the vote. "Drool for Your School" was the winner, but "Recess Serenade" was a close second. How many votes did "Drool for Your School" win by?

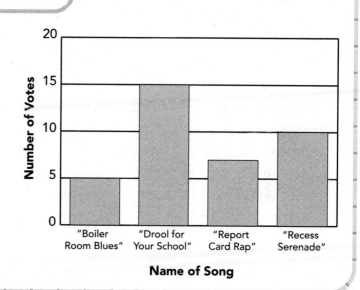

86 — Line Graphs

This graph shows how many gizingas were growing on the gizinga bush during the summer growing season. Farmer Felix invited his neighbors to pick some at the end of August. How many gizingas did they pick?

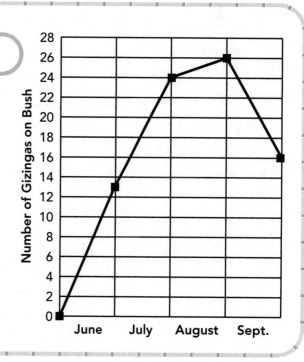

87 Pictographs

Cream Cheese and Fig on Rye	
Anchovie Panini	
Sprouts and Grapefruit on a Bagel	
Pig Knuckles on Toast	
Banana and Butter Sub	
Bacon, Squid, and Marshmallow on White	

Samantha Salamantha, the sensational sandwich maker, was charting the popularity of some of her best-known creations. Last year her best-seller was the Cream Cheese and Fig on Rye. She sold 12,000 of them. How many did she sell this year? Is it still her best-seller?

 = 10,000 sold

88 Probability

Dawgwood has a bag full of Silly Sam's Sour Suckers. In the bag, 7 are lemon flavored, 3 are ink flavored, 3 are turkey flavored, 2 are glue flavored, and 1 is toothpaste flavored. Use a fraction to describe the probability of picking a toothpaste-flavored sucker.

89   Predicting Outcomes

The hot new DJ, Rejek Ted, has a box of CDs. There were 8 by The Dumpsters, and one by Ima Kook. All of the CDs are that new style of popular music, Bing Bang. Use these words to describe the probability of picking certain CDs out of the box: *likely, unlikely, certain, impossible.*

    a. The Dumpsters
    b. Ima Kook
    c. Zorro's Sock Drawer
    d. Bing Bang

90   Exploring Solids

The scavenger hunt was almost over. Everyone was tired. Bill sat on a gallon can of juice. Bob sat on a cardboard box. Bonnie sat on a basketball. Barbie said, "All we have left to find is a cylinder. Can anyone find one?" Who should get up and hand over their seat?

91   Exploring Shapes

Shapey saw a movie about ancient Egypt. Now he wants to build his own pyramid out of cardboard. He cuts out four triangles. Does he need any other pieces? If so, what?

92   Lines and Line Segments

Fast Freda is setting up the field for the big running race. There are three runners. Freda wants each runner to go from one end of the field to the other. She is drawing lines for the runners to follow.

Her brother, Fast Freddy, says, "You better make them intersecting lines."

Her cousin, Fast Fatima says, "No! They should be parallel."

Who is right? Why?

Math Word Problems Made Easy: Grade 3   Scholastic Teaching Resources

93   Lines and Line Segments

Which of these boys was named after a
type of line: Linus Smith, Ray Ralston, or
Perimeter Jones? What does his first
name mean?

94   Exploring Angles

"I'm looking for a right angle," said
Professor Obvious. His prize student,
Osgood, handed him a book, a stop
sign, and a ball.

"One of these has some right angles,
but I don't remember which it is," said
Osgood. Which one has the right
angles?

95   Exploring Angles: Polygons

"I heard you were looking for a bird that flew away," said Daffy Dana.

"No, I'm looking for a polygon," said Brilliant Barbara.

"Yes, that's what I heard. Polly was gone," replied Dana.

"Right. Well, here's a polygon. It's a triangle. It has three sides. Do you know how many angles it has?"

What should Dana say?

96   Exploring Slides, Flips, and Turns

Wainscott looked at the arrows in this picture. "Looks like that second arrow is a flip of the first one." Is he correct?

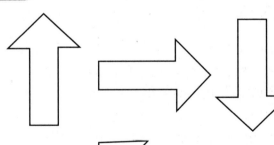
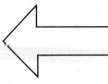
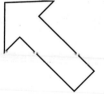

Math Word Problems Made Easy: Grade 3 · Scholastic Teaching Resources

97   Exploring Perimeter

Biff is building a pen for his new rare pet, Fuzzy the fire-breathing hamster. Fuzzy's pen has to be square. Biff measured how long he wants the first side. He wants it to be 5 feet long. What will the perimeter of the pen be?

98   Exploring Area

Peninsula has invented a new game—Banana Ball. She is drawing the lines for the court on the blacktop with chalk. It is a rectangle with a length of 10 feet and a width of 6 feet. What will the area of the court be?

Exploring Volume

Nero was using cubes to build a tower. His tower was 10 cubes wide, 2 cubes long, and 5 cubes high. His brother Caesar built a tower that was 8 cubes wide, 3 cubes long, and 5 cubes high. Which tower had the greater volume?

Exploring Perimeter and Area

Thor wants to write his name on his lawn in the backyard so it will be visible to planes and helicopters that pass over. He is cutting the letters out of the grass with his lawn mower. The area of the letter *T* is 5 square yards. What is the perimeter?

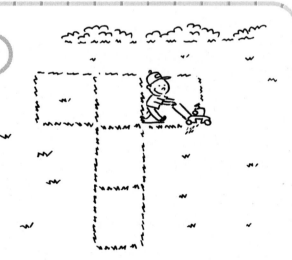

ANSWER KEY

Number and Operations

Place Value, Money, and Time

1. The Waztail

2. $3,000

3. Pat Pernicious

4. Batston

5. 1899

6. $561,200

7. Yes

8. 300,000 dust specks

9. Ms. Yelp; $10.50

10. 10:36 A.M.

11. 2 hours and 25 minutes

Addition and Subtraction

12. Pogo stick

13. 136 ants

14. 39 presents

15. A Nutto Bar and a Junior Nutto Bar

16. 365 hats

17. 9,869 feet deep

18. Yes

19. $35

20. $1.31

21. No. The correct answer is 2 dimes.

22. Yes. The quarters are only worth $4.50.

23. $14.26

24. 47¢

25. Yes. He needs 8 more badges and 2 badges x 4 weeks = 8 badges

26. 13 paper clips

27. Yes. He still has 420 marbles.

28. 48 Martians

29. 114 inches

30. 285 pieces

31. Gooey

32. 1,624 years older

33. $4.75

Multiplication and Division

34. Yes. She will have 20 spots.

35. 84 miles

36. 14 cups

37. 0 points

38. Wanda. She ate 40 bowls.

39. 78 eyes

40. 8 Garzoovians

41. 20 vitamin drops

42. 4 squid each

43. 9 spacecraft

44. 8 people

45. 5 points

46. 8 teams

47. 7 rice balls in each box

48. 9 rows

49. Rozwell has 20 bugs. Insectiva has 200 bugs. Arachnid has 2,000 bugs.

ANSWER KEY

50. No. They will need at least 3 spacecraft.

51. Merva is wrong because she said 7 x 3 would be 14. 7 x 3 = 21. Marvin will need 51 wheels.

52. 35 seven-packs

53. $78

54. 4 water buffalo

55. 1,280 inches long

56. $7.35

57. 60 minutes

58. 8 yo-yos each with 4 leftover

59. 4 peaches in each muffin

Fractions and Decimals

60. Belinda's with $\frac{1}{3}$ green icing

61. Mishy, because $\frac{1}{2}$ and $\frac{5}{10}$ are equivalent fractions

62. Pap

63. $\frac{5}{12}$

64. Yes. Miranda hit 9 targets.

65. 3 slices

66. $\frac{2}{3}$ bottle

67. $\frac{2}{4}$ or $\frac{1}{2}$

68. Jekyll

69. Ivan with a score of 9.51

70. 2.6-oz jar

71. 6.3 pounds

72. 17¢

Measurement

73. 9 inches long

74. $1\frac{1}{2}$ inches

75. $1\frac{1}{4}$ inches

76. No. The pieces would be only 48 inches.

77. 1st–Sylvester
2nd–Saliver
3rd–Socrates

78. Cletus Clamshaw

79. The one that was duct-taped together.

80. 1 more cup

81. Yes. The fountain will leak only 950 mL in five minutes, and the 1-liter bottle will hold 1,000 mL.

82. Petunia. There are 96 ounces in 6 pounds.

83. $13.50

84. Stancouver

Data Analysis and Probability

85. 5 votes

86. 10 gizingas

87. 20,000 sold this year. No, it is not the best-seller. Sprouts and Grapefruit on a Bagel is.

88. $\frac{1}{16}$

89. a. likely
b. unlikely
c. impossible
d. certain

Geometry

90. Bill

91. A square for the bottom

92. Fatima is right. Parallel lines will keep the runners from running into each other.

93. Ray Ralston. A ray is a line with only one end point.

94. The book

95. Three

96. No, it's a turn.

97. 20 feet

98. 60 square feet

99. Caesar's tower. It had a volume of 120 cubes.

100. 12 yards

TEACHER'S NOTES